Bleeding Light

poems

Sheniz Janmohamed

Dear Nasir,
Just as you have taken me on a journey through your life and ancestry, I hope these poems take you on my journey.

Inshallah! In Peace,
Shen
March 11th 2013

© 2010 Sheniz Janmohamed

Except for purposes of review, no part of this book may be reproduced in any form without prior permission of the publisher.

We acknowledge the support of the Canada Council for the Arts for our publishing program. We also acknowledge support from the Government of Ontario through the Ontario Arts Council.

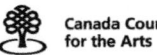 Canada Council for the Arts / Conseil des Arts du Canada 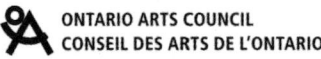 ONTARIO ARTS COUNCIL / CONSEIL DES ARTS DE L'ONTARIO

Cover art by Kushal Ghosh
Author photo by Dwayne Morgan
Design by Peggy Stockdale

"Snow Abode", "Roses are Stones" and "Sati" were previously published in *South Asian Ensemble* (Vol 2, Number 1) Winter 2010

Library and Archives Canada Cataloguing in Publication

Janmohamed, Sheniz
Bleeding light / by Sheniz Janmohamed.

ISBN 978-1-894770-63-7

I. Title.

PS8619.A6763B54 2010   C811'.6   C2010-904792-3

Printed and bound in Canada by Coach House Printing

TSAR Publications
P. O. Box 6996, Station A
Toronto, Ontario M5W 1X7
Canada

www.tsarbooks.com

Dedicated to my grandfather,
Abdul Mehdi Juma Hajee, our lion.

In memory of Kuldip Gill
and my brother, Mel Pilarski

As they
hurled stones at
the Great Sufi, Hallaj,
his friend Shibli
threw
him
a
single
red
rose

Ghazal
Arabic/Persian/Urdu/Hindi

A poetic form dating back to seventh-century Persia, consisting of couplets and a refrain, in which, traditionally, each line contains the same meter or length. In the last couplet of each ghazal, the poet often refers to him or herself.

These are not "anti-ghazals" or traditional ghazals, they are simply an attempt at maintaining the essence of the tradition and form.

Contents

The Last Cry 1
A Desert to Exchange Souls 7
Abyss of Forgetting 8
Allah-Hu 11
Light Is Bloodless 12
Upala 13
In Crimson 14
Ladders Without Rungs 15
Snow Abode 16
A Veil of Jasmine 17
The Salt of Strangling 18
Salt & Saffron 19
Restore Kismet 20
Appeasing Death 21
Haqq 25
Punctuated by Rain 26
The Lettered Palanquin 27
Naming Dukh 31
Your Infatuation Is Ishq 32
Roses Are Stones 35
Noble Soul 36
Veils 37
The Shoulder of a Lion 38
Israh Maimed 39
Bread & Lilac 40
Our Guru's Footsteps 41
Stone to Sapphire 42
Sati 43
Thunder of Monsoons 44
Bleeding Light 45
The Final Mulaqat 49
The Last Ghazal 50

The Last Cry

Ghazal: The cry of a gazelle when it is cornered by a hunter and knows it will die.

The recognition of impending death, the last cry, the moment before the arrow penetrates the heart, the wound festering, the thump of a carcass hitting the forest floor. This is the essence of a ghazal.

To write a ghazal without knowing pain reduces the writing to an academic exercise. A mastering of a literary form that has been dominated by a multiplicity of tongues—Farsi, Arabic, Urdu, Hindi, English. Are the spaces between couplets simply blank, quantum leaps between flighty ideas? No, no, the ghazal is more than this.

When I began writing ghazals in English, I was cautious. I obeyed the formal elements; I paid attention to rhyme, rhythm, meter, metaphor, refrain, the weight of each word. There is a certain discomfort in squeezing yourself into a form, like getting into new clothes. Too tight, to stiff, not enough room to move freely. But eventually, the form becomes flexible, it begins to shape around your voice, your tone—and that is when a ghazal is born. Writing ghazals in English will never be the same as writing them in the language of their origin, but like the musical experiments that occur around the ghazal, the poet can improvise and rework the form, as long as the seed is the same.

However, the stylistic elements must not be completely abandoned or forgotten. They must become imprinted in the mind, memorized in the fingers. The poet becomes the gazelle, the ghazal is her cry, and the muse is invariably her hunter. The ghazal must be exquisite in its suffering. A last beautiful whimper, as it were.

When we are dying, they say, our lives become clear. It all makes sense. Words, images, memories pass through the mind's eye seamlessly. But before a gazelle's death, there is a chase. The disorientation of the hunt, thoughts moving quicker than feet, panic, hysteria, disjunction.

The last cry, the ghazal, is the final lament. The trembling before death, the knowledge that there is no way out, that blood must be drawn, that lips will turn blue. The turning to the Light. And so the poet, in an attempt to be prolific, to remain sane, must synthesize thoughts, profound thoughts, images. Each couplet is one of these thoughts, solidified. The space between these offerings is breath.

Israh

The Takhallus
The Pen name

Glory to (Allah)
Who did take His Servant
For a Journey by night
From the Sacred Mosque
To the Farthest Mosque,
Whose precincts We did
Bless—in order that We
Might show him some
Of Our Signs: for He
Is the One Who heareth
And seeth (all things).

The Holy Qur'an
Surah al Isra
Ayat 1
(Translation by
Abdullah Yusuf Ali)

NOOR
(Arabic/Urdu)

The light which resides in each heart.
When capitalized, the Divine Light.
It cannot be extinguished.

A Desert to Exchange Souls

With one word, he can snuff out the wavering flame of our noor.
A sentence from his lips leaves us contemplating darkness in noor.

In his desert, he would exchange his soul for a mirage of floating frames.
But this desert is an oasis, and his soul is blind in the sight of her noor.

If you close your eyes, Thar's black sands will swarm your seizing lungs.
Panthers pace and howl in the night, scratching moonlight to erase noor.

They collect diamonds to capture a sliver of light with no light of its own.
Crouch naked in a lightless room. Strike the match to ignite your noor.

If no spark shimmers in the waves of the sea, she drowns in her own flood.
Israh's nib traces the steps of the night journey. Lost, she searches for Noor.

Abyss of Forgetting

She begins to compose just before dawn, when most have left
    their bodies behind.
Hearing one refrain of his suffering, her walls stiffen to ice. To melt
    is her only prayer.

If you care to be infected with mindless utterances, stroll through
    Queen's Park at night.
In that granite glow is a palimpsest of souls who remembered the
    voice of their prayer.

Left in the company of her helplessness, she picks diamonds spilling
    from his lips.
Crushing coal, she cannot blow on the flame of his light. She can only
    perform his prayer.

He shoves her into his abyss of forgetting. She kisses shadows of men
    she does not love.
When light is a myth and the attic of his mind becomes her solace,
    what use is prayer?

Who ghazals tears that never emerge? Who bottles the salt crusting
    this heart?
Israh drifts in a surfaceless sea. When she cannot sink or swim,
    she transmits prayer.

HU
(Arabic)

Allah is. God is, just He! He Himself.
A declaration. A celebration.
A recitation.

RUH
(Arabic)

Spirit.
One of the six subtleties
that must be illuminated.

Allah-Hu

He is closer to me than my jugular vein. My blood circulates Allah-Hu.
If there was no return from death, she would exist in the breath of Allah-Hu.

He paints Creation but knows his canvas still remains imperfect.
Each brushstroke copies a leaf, a bud and a branch swaying to Allah-Hu.

Drunk on the wine of the sitar, she thumps bells and spins around her ruh.
Nusrat is resurrected in every snap of her wrist, pearls fall to Allah-Hu.

When everything we create has already been created, what is innovation?
Israh's words were penned before, with ink that leaked Allah-Hu.

Light Is Bloodless

Before night falls, His breath swallows the city. These streetlights are draped in blue.
In subway carriages, papers are read and re-read. We are deaf to the cracking of our ruh.

Descending into the damp earth of her childhood, she cannot recall the scent of pines.
Clasping seeds, she sobs. She curls herself on the forest floor, drains salt from her ruh.

When he does not return, he will not return. We must not draw circles in straight paths.
Instead, let us sift sand for stars. This galaxy spins only if we learn to dance in our ruh.

He lays her down to make love to himself. She digs up rotting soil— the muck of deceit.
She must abandon him now. If she does not, she will only thirst at the shores of his ruh.

You have twisted your veins into shackles, Israh. Stop running, allow your self to sit.
Light is bloodless. Do not puncture your heart to pour light—simply drink from your ruh.

Upala

When we walk, the amber of streetlights bathes the fresh snow with opal.
He takes his hand from my garnet heart—drains blood from opal.

To separate myself from you begs the question:
How does one extract the breath of fire from an opal?

When God is a myth and your hands numb from gripping wires
The Creator's foot leaves a path of rainbows: opals.

If only words were not spiders trapped in webs of white noise
Israh would spit gems from her mouth: her tongue circling opals.

In Crimson

A man sells packets of socks in a gully where most men walk barefoot.
What can he do but rest his head on that ledge, hastily painted crimson?

In Old Town, Allah hu Akbar pounds the walls of crumbling Fort Jesus.
A taxi cuts us off, Allah is Great plastered on his window—in crimson.

At the Coast, we bargain shillings for bags and kisii stone elephants.
Indians are not good customers. The seller brands our skin crimson.

Bombs detonate at the steps of every mosque, in the throat of every believer.
If Allah is a war cry, how can we lift Bismillah from asphalt stained crimson?

If only we planted a thousand trees for each page we discard and crumple!
When her last pen snaps, Israh will draw blood and scrawl words in crimson.

Ladders Without Rungs

In deep sleep, our children sip nectar from the snow of Kashmir.
At dawn, blood soaks their bed sheets like dyed cashmere.

We have swallowed black stones washed up on the shore,
And in the heavy pit of our stomachs, we idolize our fear.

They drill oil from oceans, drag seals to slaughter, unsalt seas.
But whose hands will control the boat when there is no boat to steer?

Call the saint a fool. He welcomes death in a puddle of sunlight.
Declare the fool a saint. He refuses death until his body is revered.

Build your skyscrapers and towers, stretch your hands toward God.
Israh scales the ladder without rungs. Without rungs, the sky appears.

Snow Abode

Where the Ganga and Indus meet: the abode of the Himalayas.
To locate silence, crack the blue-laced ice of the Himalayas.

Instead of adorning Kaiser-i-Hind's royal head,
The Kohinoor should've been buried at the foot of our Himalayas.

When Sadhus utter Vedas, when Bodhisattvas turn at the gates,
We re-press buttons and glide up to our penthouse Himalayas.

Parvati of Mountains, daughter of Himavan and wife of Shiva,
Does she purse her lips and blow stars to dust the Himalayas?

We are conquerors of nothing, not the sandstorms nor the snow.
Genghis Khan could not traverse the mighty Himalayas.

When sleep numbs eyes and hands curl to stone, I will stop.
Israh's death: crushed under piles of paper Himalayas.

A Veil of Jasmine

On this death bed, hang a thick veil of jasmine.
The last breath tastes sweet, like blooming jasmine.

We have forgotten the scent of our seeds and soil.
Naipaul stuck a sprig in his buttonhole: jasmine.

If you thrust a knife into your chest, she'll know.
She'll plait her hair with blood and stringed jasmine.

The residue of light cannot be felt between the fingers.
For in the garden of a fakir, jasmine is not jasmine.

In your gathering, women only kindle the light of lanterns.
But when Israh recites, men are hushed by fire and heavy jasmine.

The Salt of Strangling

Clutch her hand, yours will enclose a glossy bangle.
Her voice laces poison, like Saturn's rings: streaked bangles.

Clarify! What for? Sand begets glass, coal glints diamond.
If we bathe ourselves in dust, in what waves will we tangle?

To witness your drowned self: the choke of salt, names gurgling.
With that ocean heaving your corpse, where does sanity dangle?

How many tongues will hang from their severed heads
If more machetes slice babies? if starry banners remain spangled?

When Israh speaks of Nothing, they will hoist her up the prison walls,
Her neck roped with seaweed. But they are the ones who strangle.

Salt & Saffron

The sea is a skin of watery gold: waves hazed saffron.
Dowse yourself until your soul prays saffron.

Before opening her chest to seal her holed heart
They rub her body with iodine: She glazes saffron.

Will I love someone enough to burn for them?
Crackling in the flames, my flesh blazes saffron.

The Queen of Egypt scattered stigma into her bath.
Fragrant water and kisses: her lovers praised saffron.

The horizon descends, plagues ravage our plains.
We pluck crocuses for God, hands raising saffron.

Israh counts her tears with strands of unread letters.
Her inked salt is more precious than phrased saffron.

Restore Kismet

He witnesses her birth in his eyes, her death on his lips. Why does he ignore kismet?
When his name blazes in her throat, she cracks the flask of time and pours kismet.

She salves wounds with wounds. It is the only way to salt her blood into indifference.
With a vial of salt in one hand and her gouged heart in the other, she deplores kismet.

He turns his back to the galaxy of her light. But she can burn him without touching.
In his eyes, her Sun is a black hole. With dusted stars on her lips, she implores kismet.

Remember to conceal your tears, Israh. Do not drink in the honey of his words.
We warn us against defeat. So we battle without swords, with no hope to restore kismet.

Appeasing Death

He cannot illuminate this darkness. She clicks her tongue to summon
the ruse of death.
Turning locked doors without keys, she manifests before him—
a cloaked muse of death.

He encourages us at the edge. Refusing to fall, we are drenched in
the web of stars.
He stumbles beneath the light. We will hurl him into dark matter
to appease Death.

Her Sufi brother claims that all things vibrate. Tune into your selves,
and you begin to sing.
If our bodies shed water and salt without crying, we cannot hear
the groan of death.

When he kisses breath out of her lungs, she deflates. She surfaces in
seas of scented ink.
Each space between words is a mirror. Her reflection will remain,
long after her death.

Unable to wield weapons or sharpen blades, she stirs her poisoned
finger in your glass.
Toxins taste sweet. If you aim your arrow at Israh, you will
surrender to your own death.

HAQQ
(Arabic)

truth.
When capitalized,
Ultimate Truth.
Al-Haqq
One of the 99 names of Allah.
The Sufi saint
Al-Hallaj uttered the words
Ana-al-Haqq
I AM THE TRUTH.
For which he was stoned,
beheaded, and burned.
His ashes were scattered
into the Tigris River,
Iraq.

Haqq

His face surfaces in every mirror; she cannot rid herself of this haqq.
She draped the glass and prayed, but could not declare ana-al-Haqq.

To forget she exists in his eyes, she numbs herself into chaotic silence.
If she walks away from him only to find him again, she unearths al-Haqq.

She rejoices as he snaps her arteries. Her body is laden with warm blood—
For to die by the sculptor's hand is to die with beauty: this is her only haqq.

Sometimes she skims his lips before he speaks, mastering the art of reading.
She flips his pages but often there are no words. So she searches him for haqq.

If you bruise her hands with kisses and break her fingers with your tongue,
Israh will breathe her name into your mouth—spelling yours with Haqq.

Punctuated by Rain

La ilaha illah Allah punctuated by rain.
The way to halt thunder is to pray for rain.

Frost was convinced the world would end in fire and ice.
But these eyes know God speaks in floods, light, and rain.

Hagar and Ishmael sunk their names in sand.
Zamzam sprouted as they cried, When will it rain?

Hallaj's ashes bloated the Tigris with Truth.
When they surface, this desert will drown in his rain.

For you, it is singed streets, locusts, blood scraping skies,
But Israh's end will come when the pen no longer reigns.

The Lettered Palanquin

In the sandstorm, he waits for her hand. She will walk; she does not need
   a palanquin.
He orients himself with the moon, she searches at dawn. He is not in
   the sun's palanquin.

Without thread to string beads of her voice, she slices her tongue—it is
   offered at his feet.
Glass light scatters with blood. He digs his heel into her mouth as she
   enters his palanquin.

There are questions pretending to be answers, and answers pretending to
   lack questions.
She asks permission to love. Will he climb out of the prison disguised
   as a palanquin?

The road is paved and unpaved. When she reaches the cul-de-sac, she will
   not turn back.
She leaves breadcrumbs in rubies. If he follows her, he'll uncover a
   rusted palanquin.

When Israh encounters Sheniz, they exhume each other—coughing words
   cut like jewels.
We adorn this page with gems. Will he bear the weight and lift this
   lettered palanquin?

DUKH
(Urdu)

Suffering, sorrow, pain.
Affliction. The anguish that
leaves a wound in the heart.
Sukh
Happiness. Bliss.

ISHQ
(Arabic/Urdu)

Love without lust
Ishq-e-majazi
The spark
between a man and a woman
spreading like a river of flames
toward
Divine Love
Ishq-e-Haqiqi

Naming Dukh

We'll dance until the ice cracks. Hoard your breath, drown in dukh.
Each refrain splits an artery. So bleed, bleed in the ecstasy of this dukh!

He asks for a match. She gifts him a torch, and witnesses herself burn.
Sleeping in flames, she is reduced to ash. He smears her heart with dukh.

You are afraid to fall. Only a coward blinds himself from the light of ishq.
I have fallen, I have lost. My neck breaks from hanging myself with dukh.

We are strangers. We are strangers who recognize our selves in each other.
What reason is there to meet? No reason left but for her to admit her dukh.

Israh turns to him to ask, how do you name love that cannot name itself?
He has no answer, she has no response. So she drags herself through dukh.

Your Infatuation Is Ishq

Inspired by *The Body of My Garden* by Rishma Dunlop

Leaning over a table in a sun-filtered room, she waits. Her pen scribbles
    his name—she writes ishq.
When you've lost the will to eat, your heart starves. Fast! Gladly suffer
    the hunger of ishq.

Where has he disappeared? He directs the words and actions of others,
    but forgets his own.
My beloved is married to a vision that kills. I would load the bullets if
    he only admitted his ishq.

We met by the Body of My Garden, our souls immediately recognizing
    our eyes. Paper flowers seemed real.
You've trampled these flowers and stamped them in mud. I search
    your face, for just one seed of ishq.

Do you recall the taste of her scented skin? The burnt rose blooming at
    the tip of your tongue?
She hears herself in your voice, under the veils of pretense. Plead sober
    —but you are drunk with ishq.

Time stalls for Israh, so do not flip the hourglass. The sand will not
    drain until you satisfy your thirst.
Israh makes this promise: suspend your art for one minute, and you'll
    live a century in her ishq.

FANAA'
(Arabic/Urdu)

Annihilation
of the self,
The ego.
Passing Away
in God.
Union with the One.
The poet Attar likened Fanaa' to the mystical flying bird,
the Simurgh.
30 birds in One.
A mirror of One
in the reflection of All.
Baqa'
subsistence in God,
the final
stage.

Roses Are Stones

Beckoned in his dream, the Saint abandoned his house. Now he
    drones in dust, in dust.
On the day of your birth, Sufis swirl into Hu. If you refuse, I will
    follow them to fanaa'.

Hazrat Ali's emerald robe is drenched in sand. Her forehead yearns to
    touch his feet.
The desert grit grates her teeth. If blood spills in the land of poppies,
    where is fanaa'?

Can a ghazal transform into a qawwali? One voice cannot raise
    the bones of this grief.
If her hands crack from clapping, she will seek out the Simurgh.
    Wings sprout in fanaa'.

How many stones will you throw before you claim her a heretic?
    Your stones are roses.
With roses, she self-flagellates. Your breath in my breath is
    the closest breath to fanaa'.

If dukh had a name, it would be Israh. Even sukh tastes like a dukh
    she cannot swallow.
We are an amalgamation of stars. When every star implodes,
    we will attain our fanaa'.

Noble Soul

Common lovers call their beloved my other half.
But I am you, how can there be a half in a whole?

A marriage of souls cannot be named a union.
A union was once separation. But a diamond is coal.

In my veins runs your blood. When you hurt, I bruise.
My eyes are yours. I sign your name with my kohl.

I see you in the mirror. I'm vain for your love.
If the glass cracks, time repents for the seconds it stole.

This poem is your talisman. Wear it like a cloak of stars.
I will stitch you a galaxy for every black hole.

Israh fears your death more than her own.
Do not die for her. Live for her, Noble Soul.

Veils

These eyes penetrate the mirror and I lose my face.
To be alone is to unearth what we cannot face.

If glass fails to recollect then I no longer exist
Ink betrays while the page lays down its face.

If the city were an orb, there would be no exit,
Only ringed footsteps littering a concrete face.

Think of death everyday, Sufis warn the flock.
While Death scratches the paint off our face.

Taste my hair, your tongue will bloom jasmine.
Its rotting buds float under the screen of my face.

And where there is sand, there is the Prophet's voice.
His mouth laces Arabic, relics cannot reveal his face.

If this city were an orb, there would be an exit without return.
Israh crouching by a streetlight, veils flaking from her face.

The Shoulder of a Lion

The Rift Valley in these veins, our house occupied
    by lions.
Her great great grandfather had no ordinary pets.
    He encaged lions.

The family is riddled with them, those beasts with matted manes,
    those beasts.
Hazrat Ali sharpened his sword in desert battles, in our books
    he was the lion.

If you stand alone in Tsavo, in the blotted blue night,
    you will hear them grunt.
You will see the smoke-laced shadow, his body
    the breath of a lion.

His father, hurricane lamp in hand, sent through the woods
    to the train station.
Knocked at the station door, two dead, his flesh saved
    from man-eating lions.

She had a dream once. Of a lion slouching towards her, rain slanting
    the grey sky.
The seer explained: A male lion is a symbol of female strength.
    A male lion.

These fingers stroke the face in the mirror, for the scent of
    damp fur, a tuft even.
Claw for a clot of blood, Israh, in the Rift Valley.
    In the shoulder of a lion.

Israh Maimed

Blood and rain mingle, the sun remains a pariah.
without knives and torn flags, who can tame a pariah?

The Book cracks to resurrect sand into Arabic.
Before crowned, the Prophet was claimed a pariah.

The bruise of dawn pools itself and spreads onto concrete.
In these city sirens, God is named a pariah.

Latte in her hand, gripping the World Affairs section
Islam, Iraq, Afghanistan, who isn't blamed a pariah?

This pen unravels veins, jabs its nib into her blood.
She's cast her shadow, Israh maimed: a pariah.

Bread & Lilac

In the razed sea, the Varkala sun is suffused with lilac.
With limbs choking the shore, what beauty are hands bruised lilac?

If Eliot shoveled his pen through our wasted Wasteland,
He would dig up dirt and dead leaves to find abused lilacs.

Young Turks plucked its stems to sculpt pipes, puffing tar and smoke.
To be hollowed with black muck leaves for a confused lilac.

For Carl Sandburg, poetry is biscuits and hyacinths.
But if he only had bread, would he have refused lilac?

If Israh's letters were hues and the horizon her paper,
She would mingle blue with dusk and inhale infused lilac.

Our Guru's Footsteps

For Kuldip Gill

To honour your nemesis is to place wreaths at the feet of your guru.
Who will children love to fear if the world empties itself of gurus?

She appears to have a European mind, lined with pages of Shelley.
But she prays on carpet and covers her head to respect her guru.

At midnight, drive to Nandi Hills. Tune in to thousands of cicadas.
When mist lifts from the road, kiss the ground. You kiss your guru.

We take steps without sight, huddle by the lamp that bears no light.
How can we walk the path without the candle of our beloved guru?

If seeds are meant to take root, they should grow in the shadow of a tree.
To scatter petals on the page, Israh must enter the garden of her guru.

Stone to Sapphire

The fragrance between your fingers is the smoke
    of my entire being.
Let me burn in the flames of your intoxication.
    I am nothing but fire.

From your hands, rose petals fall. Where is the garden
    of your splendour?
I search the soil at your feet to find nothing.
    But this seeker will never tire.

Your imperfections are beautiful in their imperfection.
    This is perfection.
There is alchemy in your honeyed eyes: One glance
    and stone turns to sapphire!

Others ask for proof. Israh does not need to see the crown to know
    the King exists.
What is unseen is seen. Each galaxy is a pearl strung into
    the necklace of Our Sire.

Sati

She refused to wear gold, simple saris groomed a widow.
A woman whose eyes do not smile must be presumed a widow.

To Southey, our Hindi was the chattering of baboons.
While he defecated on the words of poets and perfumed widows.

They strung Hobson-Jobson from cries of Ya Hasan! Ya Husain!
And in the dust of Karbala, the martyr's blood bloomed widows.

We dyed their indigo, weaved their paisley, plucked their precious tea.
They defiled our soil, and to our land, we were assumed widows.

The page is my beloved, all other lovers are liars.
If the word died tonight, Israh would be infumed: a widow.

Thunder of Monsoons

How can an umbrella shield us from this media monsoon?
We're still wet, though we've shut off the digital monsoon.

He claims to channel the light and speech of thunderstorms.
But his lips dribble venom, coated with the dew of monsoons.

Her compass slips overboard, her boat swells with seawater.
Yet she continues to paddle into the rainy sheen of a monsoon.

On the next ark, prepare for bomb sniffer dogs and metal detectors.
What would Noah do if no dove arrived? Call for another monsoon?

In this room of mirrors and smoke, the ceiling is only a screen of stars.
When Israh greets with her salaam, listen for the thunder of monsoons.

Bleeding Light

With your breath in her lungs, she dies with every exhalation.
If only she could inhale without exhaling, she would live by dying.

The ground is not low enough to prostrate before Him.
How can her candle flicker in the Sun? This fire is undying.

Her throat must be dry to know thirst. Every drop is an ocean.
To drink without a cup is to shed tears without crying.

Only the pen knows how to draw blood without bleeding.
When every vein fills with Light, Israh will stop sighing.

MULAQAT
(Urdu)

A meeting of man and woman, of soul and spirit.
When capitalized, the meeting of the lover with the Beloved.
A secret meeting, a sacred meeting, a brief meeting.
A meeting of the poetess with her page,
the performer with her audience
the music with lyrics.

The Final Mulaqat

How can we smoke the opium of sleep? Ink and paper demand
    a midnight mulaqat.
The gold of our perfume lingers—long after these patrons depart
    from our mulaqat.

He refrains from this refrain. Ignoring her scrawling whisper, he forgets
    his own voice.
She bangs his door. Her knuckles bleed. But he has not earned the right
    of her mulaqat.

Who will shatter mirrors but herself? She ingests shards. Light bleeds
    from her mouth.
To live, she dies first. Death does not appear if the blade and soul
    have their mulaqat.

Blossoms adorn the pavement, the traffic stalls. Dawn has swept this city
    into silence.
It is the silence before thunder, before rain. In a shock of light, we have
    His Mulaqat.

Praise your eyes! You have skimmed the braille of her skin. She pins
    roses to your heart.
Israh's ink dries itself in dusk. Her last request: untie the ribbons
    of this blessed mulaqat.

The Last Ghazal

Have you collected her pearls and strung them into the necklace
  of each ghazal?
Which one will wedge itself in the funnel of your throat—the first
  or final ghazal?

This page is a prayer mat. I will count beads and prostrate until
  my spine snaps.
Soil is not enough. Words stitched with stars must weave a ghazal
  to end ghazals.

In the glass, she is her child. The scent of her tears is the pink mist
  of a dying dusk.
Dawn refuses to return. She cannot write letters to herself, not
  in this lone ghazal.

Do you know the simplicity of a red leaf? The dew lingering on
  a blade of grass?
She surrenders to the forest. Her breath nestles itself in the wings
  of this ghazal.

When the gazelle dies, we die. Drop the bow, retract the arrow
  and weep. Weep!
If Israh does not squeeze the valves of your heart, how can we claim
  to be a ghazal?

Acknowledgements

My mom, Nigar, for planting the seed of Sufism in my heart.
My dad, Abdul, for playing ghazals until I learned to love them.
My dad, Joseph, for having more faith in me than I do in myself.
My sister, Aleeza, for bailing me out, driving me around, cheering me on.

The Janmohamed family, the Hajee family and the Pilarski family for your support, well wishes, encouragement and inspiration.

The girls and staff of Loretto College.

Diana Kryski.

Binish Ahmed, for lending me your Agha Shahid Ali book and introducing me to the world of ghazals in English.

Yousuf Arain and Saima Yousuf, my brother and sister—Blood turns to water when there is light between souls. Thank you.

Jehanzeb Dar—There is no distance between kindred spirits.

Anita Majumdar, for your insight, honesty, constant support and guidance.

The students and staff of the MFA program at the University of Guelph.

Dionne Brand.
Connie Rooke, you are missed.
Janice Kulyk Keefer.
Sandy Pool.

Tricia Postle, for being the first to produce a show of my ghazals.
Tanya Jacobs, for putting my ghazals to beautiful music.
Kushal Ghosh, for the stunning cover image.

My teachers and professors.

Agha Shahid Ali, for leaving a trail for us to follow.

Nurjehan Aziz and MG Vassanji, for taking a risk on me.

My guide lives many mountains away, but he is visible before me
—Sultan Bahu